Questions Jesus Asked:
Leader Guide

Questions Jesus Asked

Questions Jesus Asked
978-1-7910-2688-2
978-1-7910-2782-7 *eBook*

Questions Jesus Asked: DVD
978-1-7910-2785-8

Questions Jesus Asked: Leader Guide
978-1-7910-2783-4
978-1-7910-2784-2 *eBook*

Also by Magrey R. deVega

Awaiting the Already:
An Advent Journey Through the Gospels

Embracing the Uncertain:
A Lenten Study for Unsteady Timest

Savior:
What the Bible Says about the Cross

The Bible Year:
A Journey Through Scripture in 365 Days

With April Casperson, Ingrid McIntyre, and Matt Rawle
Almost Christmas:
A Wesleyan Advent Experience

MAGREY R. DEVEGA

Questions JesusASKED

Leader Guide

by Clara Welch

Abingdon Press | Nashville

Questions Jesus Asked:
Leader Guide

Copyright © 2023 Abingdon Press
All rights reserved.

978-1-7910-2783-4

MANUFACTURED IN THE
UNITED STATES OF AMERICA

TO THE LEADER

Welcome! Thank you for accepting the invitation to serve as the facilitator for this study of *Questions Jesus Asked* by Magrey R. deVega. You and your group of learners will journey together toward a greater understanding of the meaning behind six of the questions that Jesus asked when he walked this earth. These are timeless questions and ones that require our careful attention if we want to grow into a deeper faith and closer relationship with Jesus Christ.

This six-session study includes the following components:

- the book *Questions Jesus Asked* by Magrey R. deVega
- this Leader Guide
- a DVD with video segments for each of the six chapters in the book

It will be helpful if participants obtain a copy of the book in advance and read chapter 1 before the first session. Each participant will need a Bible. It is recommended that each participant also have a notebook or journal for taking notes, recording insights, and noting questions during the study.

Session Format

Every group is different. These session plans have been designed to give you flexibility and choices. A variety of activities and discussion questions are included. As you plan each session, keep the session goals in mind and select the activities and discussion questions that will be most meaningful for your group.

Read the section titled "Before the Session" several days in advance of your meeting time. A few activities suggest making some preparations in advance.

In many cases your session time will be too short to do everything that is suggested here. Select activities and questions that best fit the personality of the group ahead of time. Decide how much time you want to allow for each part of the session plan.

Each session plan follows this outline.

Planning the Session
- Session Goals
- Biblical Foundation

Before the Session
- Getting Started
- Greetings and Introductions
- Leading into the Study
- Opening Prayer

Learning Together
- Video Study and Discussion
- Bible Study and Discussion
- Book Study and Discussion
- Optional Activity

Wrapping Up
- Closing Activity
- Closing Prayer

Preparing for the Session

- Pray for the leading of the Holy Spirit as you prepare for the study. Pray for discernment for yourself and for each member of the study group.
- Before each session, familiarize yourself with the content. Read the book chapter again and watch the video segment. Read the Scripture passages that support each lesson. Feel free to consult different translations.
- Read through the lesson plan; then go back and choose the activities and questions you wish to use during the session. Plan carefully, yet also be prepared to adjust the session as group members interact and questions arise. Allow space for the Holy Spirit to move in and through the material, the group members, and you as facilitator.
- Secure in advance a TV and DVD player or a computer with projection.

- Prepare the space so it will enhance the learning process. Ideally, group members should be seated around a table or in a circle so they can see one another. Movable chairs are best so participants may easily form pairs or small groups for discussion.
- Bring a supply of Bibles for those who forget to bring their own. Having a variety of translations is helpful.
- For each session you will also need a whiteboard and markers, a chalkboard and chalk, or an easel with paper and markers.

Shaping the Learning Environment

- Begin and end on time.
- Create a climate of openness, encouraging group members to participate as they feel comfortable. Remember that some people will jump right in with answers and comments, while others will need time to process what is being discussed.
- If you notice that some group members don't enter the conversation, ask them if they have thoughts to share. Give everyone a chance to talk, but keep the conversation moving. Try to prevent a few individuals from doing all the talking.
- Communicate the importance of group discussions and group activities.
- If no one answers at first during discussions, don't be afraid of pauses. Count silently to ten; then say something such as "Would anyone like to go first?" If no one responds, venture an answer yourself and ask for comments.
- Model openness as you share with the group. Group members will follow your example. If you limit your sharing to a surface level, others will follow suit.
- Encourage multiple answers or responses before moving on.
- Ask, "Why?" or "Why do you believe that?" or "Can you say more about that?" to help continue a discussion and give it greater depth.
- Affirm others' responses with comments such as "Great" or "Thanks" or "Good insight."
- Monitor your own contributions. If you find yourself doing most of the talking, back off so you don't train the group to listen rather than speak up.
- Remember that you don't have all the answers. Your job is to keep the discussion going and encourage participation.

Managing the Session

- Honor the time schedule. If a session is running longer than expected, get consensus from the group before continuing beyond the agreed-upon ending time.
- Involve group members in various aspects of the group session, such as playing the DVD, saying prayers, or reading the Scripture.
- Note that the session plans sometimes call for breaking into smaller groups. This gives everyone a chance to speak and participate fully. Mix up the teams; don't let the same people pair up on every activity.
- Because many activities call for personal sharing, confidentiality is essential. Group members should never pass along stories that have been shared in the group. Remind the group members at each session: confidentiality is crucial to the success of this study.

Adapting for Virtual Small Group Sessions

Meeting online is a great option for a number of situations. During a time of a public-health hazard, such as the COVID-19 pandemic, online meetings are a welcome opportunity for people to converse while seeing each other's faces. Online meetings can also expand the "neighborhood" of possible group members, because people can log in from just about anywhere in the world. This also gives those who do not have access to transportation or who prefer not to travel at certain times of day the chance to participate.

The following guidelines will help you lead an effective and enriching group study using an online video conferencing platform such as Zoom, Webex, Google Meet, Microsoft Teams, or another virtual meeting platform of your choice.

Basic Features for Virtual Meetings

There are many choices for videoconferencing platforms. You may have personal experience and comfort using a particular service, or your church may have a subscription that will influence your choice. Whichever option you choose, it is recommended that you use a platform that supports the following features:

- **Synchronous video and audio:** Your participants can see and speak to each other live, in real time. Participants have the ability to turn their video off and on and to mute and unmute their audio.
- **Chat:** Your participants can send text messages to the whole group or individuals from within the virtual meeting. Participants can put active hyperlinks (that is,, "clickable" internet addresses) into the chat for other participants' convenience.
- **Screen Sharing:** Participants can share the contents of their screen with other participants (the meeting host's permission may be required).
- **Video Sharing:** Participants (or the host) can share videos and computer audio via screen share so that all participants can view the videos each week.
- **Breakout Rooms:** Meeting hosts can automatically or manually send participants into virtual smaller groups and can determine whether the rooms end automatically after a set period of time. Hosts can communicate with all breakout rooms. *This feature is useful if your group is large, or if you wish to break into smaller teams of two or three for certain activities. If you have a smaller group, this feature may not be necessary.*

Check with your pastor or director of discipleship to see if your church has a preferred platform or an account with one or more of these platforms that you might use. In most instances, only the host will need to be signed in to the account; others can participate without being registered.

Zoom, Webex, Google Meet, and Microsoft Teams all offer free versions of their platform, which you can use if your church doesn't have an account. However, there may be some restrictions (for instance, Zoom's free version limits meetings to forty-five minutes). Check each platform's website to be sure you are aware of any such restrictions before you sign up.

Once you have selected a platform, familiarize yourself with all of its features and controls so you can facilitate virtual meetings comfortably. The platform's website will have lists of features and helpful tutorials; often, third-party sites will have useful information or instructions as well.

There are additional features on many platforms that help play your video more effectively. In Zoom, for example, as you click the "share screen" option and see the screen showing your different windows, check at the bottom of that window to choose "optimize for video clips" and "share audio." These ensure that your group hears the audio and that when using a clip, the video resolution is compressed to fit the bandwidth that you have.

In addition to videoconferencing software, it is also advisable to have access to slide-creation software such as Microsoft PowerPoint or Google Slides. These can be used to prepare easy slides for screen-sharing to display discussion questions, quotes from the study book, or Scripture passages. If you don't have easy access to these, you can create a document and share it—but make sure the print size is easy to read.

Video Sharing

For a video-based study, it's important to be able to screen-share your videos so that all participants can view them in your study session. The good news is, whether you have the videos on DVD or streaming files, it is possible to play them in your session.

All of the videoconferencing platforms mentioned above support screen-sharing videos. Some have specific requirements for assuring that sound will play clearly in addition to the videos. Follow your videoconferencing platform instructions carefully, and test the video sharing in advance to be sure it works.

If you wish to screen-share a DVD video, you may need to use a different media player. Some media players will not allow you to share your screen when you play copyright-protected DVDs. VLC is a free media player that is safe and easy to use. To try this software, download it at videolan.org/VLC.

What about copyright? DVDs like those you use for group study are meant to be used in a group setting in "real time." That is, whether you meet in person, online, or in a hybrid setting, Abingdon Press encourages use of your DVD or streaming video.

What is allowed: Streaming an Abingdon DVD over Zoom, Teams, or similar platform during a small group session.

What is not allowed: Posting video of a published DVD study to social media or YouTube for later viewing.

If you have any questions about permissions and copyright, email permissions@abingdonpress.com.

Amplify Media. The streaming subscription platform Amplify Media makes it easy to share streaming videos for groups. When your church has an Amplify subscription, your group members can sign on and have access to the video sessions. With access, they may watch the video on their own ahead of your group meeting, watch the streaming video during your group meeting, or view it again after the meeting. Thousands of videos are on AmplifyMedia.com, making it easy to watch anytime, anywhere, and on any device, from phones and tablets to Smart TVs and desktops.

Visit AmplifyMedia.com to learn more, or call 1-800-672-1789, option 4, to hear about the current offers.

Communicating with Your Group

Clear communication with your small group before and throughout your study is crucial no matter how you meet, but it is doubly important if you are gathering virtually.

Advertising the Study. Be sure to advertise your virtual study on your church's website and/or in its newsletter, as well as any social media your church uses. Request that pastors or other worship leaders announce it in worship services.

Registration. Encourage people to register for the online study so that you can know all participants and have a way to contact them. Ideally, you will collect an email address for each participant so that you can send communications and links to your virtual meeting sessions. An event planning tool such as SignUpGenius makes this easy and gives you a database of participants and their email addresses.

Welcome Email. Before your first session, several days in advance, send an email to everyone who has registered for the study, welcoming participants to the group, reminding them of the date and time of your first meeting, and including a link to join the virtual meeting. It's also a good idea to include one or two discussion questions to prime the pump for reflection and conversation when you gather.

If you have members without internet service, or if they are uncomfortable using a computer and videoconferencing software, let them know they may telephone in to the meeting. Provide them the number and let them know there is usually a unique phone number for each meeting.

Weekly Emails. Send a new email two or three days before each week's session, again including the link to join your virtual meeting and one or two discussion questions to set the stage for conversation. Feel free to use any of the questions in the Leader Guide for this purpose. If you find a particular quote from the book that is especially meaningful, include this as well.

Facebook. Consider creating a private Facebook group for your small group, where you can hold discussion and invite reflection between your weekly meetings. Each week, post one or two quotes from the study book along with a short question for reflection, and invite people to respond in the comments. These questions can come straight from the Leader Guide, and you can revisit the Facebook conversation during your virtual meeting.

You might also consider posting these quotes and questions on your church's main Facebook page, inviting people in your congregation to join the conversation beyond your small group. This can be a great way to involve others in your study, or to let people know about it and invite them to join your next virtual meeting.

During Your Virtual Sessions

During your virtual sessions, follow these tips to be sure you are prepared and that everything runs as smoothly as possible.

Getting Ready

- Familiarize yourself with the controls and features of your video-conferencing platform, using instructions or tutorials available via the platform's website or third-party sites.
- Be sure you are leading the session from a well-lit place in front of a background free from excessive distractions.
- As leader, log in to the virtual meeting early. You want to be a good host who is present to welcome participants by name as they arrive. This also gives you time to check how you appear on camera, so you can make any last-minute adjustments to your lighting and background if needed.

Creating Community Online

- During each session, pay attention to who is speaking and who is not. Because of video and audio lags as well as internet connections of varying quality, some participants may inadvertently speak over each other without realizing they are doing so. As needed, directly prompt specific people to speak if they wish (for example, "Alan, it looked like you were about to say something when Sarah was speaking").

- If your group is especially large, you may want to agree with members on a procedure for being recognized to speak (for example, participants might "raise hands" digitally or type "call on me" in the chat feature).
- Instruct participants to keep their microphones muted during the meeting, so extraneous noise from their location does not interrupt the meeting. This includes chewing or yawning sounds, which can be embarrassing! When it is time for discussion, participants can unmute themselves.
- Remember that some participants may wish to simply observe and listen—do not pressure anyone to speak who does not wish to.
- Always get your group's permission before recording your online sessions. While those who are unable to attend the meeting may appreciate the chance to view it later, respect the privacy of your participants.
- Communicate with your group in between sessions with weekly emails and Facebook posts to spark ongoing discussion.

In challenging times, modern technology has powerful potential to bring God's people together in new and nourishing ways. May such be your experience during this virtual study.

Help, Support, and Tutorials

The creators of the most popular virtual meeting platforms have excellent, free resources available online to help you get started using their platform, which teach you everything from how to join a meeting as a participant to how to use the more advanced features, like video sharing and breakout rooms. Most of them offer clear written instructions as well as video tutorials and also provide a way to contact the company in case you need additional assistance.

Following are links for five platforms: Zoom, Microsoft Teams, Webex, Google Meet, and GoTo Meeting. If you are using a different platform, go to their website and look for the "Help" or "Resources" page.

Zoom Help Center: https://support.zoom.us/hc/en-us
Contains a comprehensive collection of resources to help you use the Zoom platform, including quick start guides, video tutorials, articles, and specific sets of instructions on various topics or issues you may run into.

Microsoft Teams Help & Learning:
https://support.microsoft.com/en-us/teams
A collection of articles, videos, and instructions on how to use the Microsoft Teams platform. Teams offers a number of features. You are most likely to find the help you need for group meetings by navigating to the "Meetings" page or by clicking "Microsoft Teams training" under "Explore Microsoft Teams."

Webex Help Center: https://help.webex.com/en-us/
Contains articles, videos, and other resources to help you use the Webex platform, with everything from joining the meeting to screen-sharing and using a virtual whiteboard.

Google Meet Help: https://support.google.com/meet/
Contains a directory of support topics to help you use the Google Meet platform, in an easy-to-read expandable list that makes it easy to find just what you need.

GoTo Meeting Support: https://support.goto.com/meeting
Here you'll find links with instructions on various topics to help you use the GoTo Meeting platform.

General How-To

In addition to these official support pages, there are numerous independent sites online with great, clear instructions on using multiple platforms. Here is one excellent resource:

Nerds Chalk: https://nerdschalk.com/
This site is easily searchable and contains numerous articles and how-go guides, with clear titles to help you find exactly what you need. Simply search for your chosen platform and/or what you are trying to accomplish, such as "Breakout rooms" or "Zoom screen share," and navigate to the most relevant link.

SESSION 1

Who Do You Say That I Am?

Planning the Session

Session Goals

Through conversation, activities, and reflection, participants will consider these three questions from chapter 1:

- Who do you say Jesus is...every day?
- Who do you say Jesus is *now*?
- What difference does your answer make in your life?

Biblical Foundation

Luke 9:18-27

Before the Session

- Set up a table in the room with nametags, markers, Bibles, extra copies of *Questions Jesus Asked*, and a stack of three-by-five cards.
- Prepare a sign-in and attendance sheet with space for each participant to write his or her name and contact information.
- On a whiteboard, chalkboard, or large piece of chart paper, draw two large circles of equal size. If possible, use a different color marker or chalk for each circle. In one circle write the word *theology*. In the other circle write the words *significant event*.
- Read the Optional Activity and decide if you want to include it in your lesson plan.

Getting Started

Introductions

Greet participants as they arrive. Invite each to make a nametag, pick up a three-by-five card, and also pick up a Bible and/or copy of *Questions Jesus Asked* if needed.

Welcome participants and introduce yourself. Share why you are excited about facilitating this study of *Questions Jesus Asked*.

Invite participants to introduce themselves and share a reason why they want to participate in this study. If your group includes participants who do not have a church home, invite them to worship with your congregation.

Housekeeping

- Share any necessary information about your meeting space, parking, and the class schedule.
- Collect contact information from each participant in case you need to share information between the sessions, and also share your contact information with participants.
- Let participants know you will be faithful to the time, and encourage everyone to arrive on time.
- Encourage participants to read the upcoming chapter before the next session.
- You may want to invite participants to have a notebook, journal, or electronic tablet for use during this study. Explain that these can be used to record questions and insights they have as they read each chapter and to take notes during each session.
- Ask participants to covenant together to respect a policy of confidentiality within the group.

Leading into the Study

Share information from the introduction to *Questions Jesus Asked*, including:

- three types of questions Jesus asked:
  - ◊ factual
  - ◊ interpretative
  - ◊ evaluative

- the six questions that are the focus of this study. (Invite participants to turn to the Contents to see the list.)

Read the last paragraph of the introduction in *Questions Jesus Asked*.
Ask these "Questions for Reflection" at the end of the introduction.
Write responses to the last two questions on a large sheet of chart paper.
Keep the paper to refer back to during the last session.

- What have been the biggest and toughest questions you have had to answer in your life?
- How did answering these questions become defining moments for you?
- How easy or difficult is it for you to ask questions of your own faith?
- What concerns do you bring to this survey of questions Jesus asks of you?
- What do you hope emerges from this study for spiritual life and your commitment to Jesus?

Opening Prayer

Loving God, thank you for the gift of this day. Thank you for the gift of this time of study and fellowship together. Thank you for the gift of Jesus Christ, who continues to ask us, "Who do you say that I am?" Be with us as we journey together. Help us support one another as we all seek answers to this question. Help us be faithful followers. Let our faith make a difference in our lives so we may make a difference in your name in the lives of others. In the name of your Son, Jesus, we pray. Amen.

Learning Together

Video Study and Discussion (optional)

Invite the group to consider these three questions as they view the video:

- What questions did you ask as a child?
- Magrey de Vega says that after we confess that Jesus is the Christ or Messiah our story is still incomplete. Why?
- What does it mean to you to commit your life to following Jesus as the Christ and Messiah?

Following the video, invite volunteers to share their responses to the questions above.

Bible Study and Discussion: Luke 9:18-27

Read or invite a volunteer to read the first two verses of the Biblical Foundation Scripture, Luke 9:18-19.

Highlight these Key Points from *Questions Jesus Asked*:

- This conversation between Jesus and his disciples is reported in three Gospels: Matthew 16:13-28, Mark 8:27-38, and Luke 9:18-27.
- In the Gospel of Luke, this conversation takes place during a quiet time for Jesus, "when Jesus was praying by himself" (Luke 9:18).
- In contrast, Matthew and Mark set the conversation during a busy time for Jesus and in a busy place, "the area of Caesarea Philippi" (Matthew 16:13) and "the villages near Caesarea Philippi" (Mark 8:27).
- In the Gospels of Luke, Matthew, and Mark, another key event, the transfiguration of Jesus, takes place shortly after this discussion between Jesus and his disciples.

Ask:

- How did the disciples answer Jesus's first question in this Scripture passage, "Who do the crowds say that I am?"
- In what ways was Jesus like John the Baptist? (*Jesus called people to repentance and a new way of life.*)
- In what ways was Jesus like Elijah? (*Jesus challenged the powerful and aided the poor.*)
- In what ways was Jesus like the ancient prophets? (*Jesus spoke for God and called people to faithful obedience.*)
- How was Jesus more than John the Baptist, Elijah, and the ancient prophets?

Read Jesus's second question and Peter's response in Luke 9:20. Call attention to these key points from *Questions Jesus Asked*:

- The Greek word *Christ* and the Hebrew word *Messiah* both mean "anointed one."

- In that day, kings were anointed.
- Many first-century Jews held an expectation that God would send *the* Messiah, "the Christ" who was anointed and "sent from God," who would usher in God's kingdom.
- With this statement Peter was beginning to understand the mystery that Jesus "the Christ" is God.

Ask:

- Why does deVega suggest that Peter's "right answer" was not the "complete answer" regarding our understanding of Jesus?

Read or invite a volunteer to read the remaining verses of the Biblical Foundation Scripture, Luke 9:21-27. **Ask:**

- What is the most important lesson you learn from these verses about what it means for you to follow Jesus?

Book Study and Discussion

Magrey R. deVega suggests three questions for us to consider as we answer Jesus's question, "Who do you say that I am?" These questions are listed as the goals for this session. This Book Study and Discussion will focus on these three questions.

Call attention to the first question: **Who do you say Jesus is...every day?**

Read this quote from the section "The Journey Is Part of the Answer": "It's one thing to demonstrate what one knows about Jesus. It is quite another to discover who one is in relation to that Jesus every day."

Read John Wesley's direction to "resolve to be faithful. Having engaged your hearts, opened your mouths, and subscribed with your hands to the Lord, resolve in his strength never to go back."

Ask:

- Who do you say Jesus is . . . every day?
- How do you resolve to remain faithful every day?
- What might tempt you to turn away from Christ?
- What helps you remain focused and faithful to following Christ?

Call attention to the second question: **Who do you say Jesus is now?**

Read this quote from the section "Allowing Our Relationships to Change": "God can use our experiences to open our eyes to deeper, richer ways to see Jesus, and renew our faith in him."

Show the group the circles drawn on the board or chart paper with the words *theology* and *significant event* (see "Before the Session"). Write responses to the following questions in and around the appropriate circle.

Ask:

- What does theology include? (Responses will center around beliefs about who God is.)
- What significant life events have prompted you to be mindful of God's presence and activity in your life?

Share information about the three paradigms, or models, de Vega references in the section "Allowing Our Relationships to Change." Note that these three models help provide insight into the relationship between beliefs about God and life experiences.

- Paradigm 1: The circles are the same size. "Everything makes sense."
- Paradigm 2: The theology circle is wider. Is God calling us to see or learn more?
- Paradigm 3: The significant event circle is wider. Is our understanding of God too narrow or restricted?

Ask these "Questions for Reflection" from the end of chapter 1 of *Questions Jesus Asked:*

- When do you remember first pondering the question of who Jesus is to you?
- When have there been times when your circle of life experience has matched up perfectly with the circle of your theology?
- When has there been tension between those two circles?
- In what ways did those tensions push you to grow and see both yourself and God in a more nuanced, mature way?

Invite participants to turn to the section "Expanding Our Theology of Prayer."

Note the different images the author has had of Jesus, for example, royalty on the throne, "a cosmic vending machine," and a friend.

Ask:

- How do you picture Jesus or God when you pray?
- How has your understanding of who God is changed over time?
- How has your understanding and experience of prayer changed as you have matured in your faith?
- When have you experienced times of drought in your prayer life?
- What helped you move past these times?
- What questions and longings do you have now related to your life of prayer with the Lord?

Remind the group of Jesus's question, "Who do you say that I am?"

Then ask the third question, **What difference does your answer make in your life?**

Ask:

- Who are people for whom a faithful relationship with Jesus Christ made a big difference in their lives? (Responses may include famous men and women of faith, people in your congregation, family members, and friends.)
- How did their lives of faith impact other people, their community, and/or the world?
- How has your answer to the question "Who do you say that I am?" changed over time?
- What difference has your faith in Christ made in your life and does it continue to make in your life?

Optional Activity: Discussing Luke 4:18-19

Read or invite a volunteer to read Luke 4:18-19. This is printed in *Questions Jesus Asked.*

Ask:

- What does this passage of Scripture tell us about Jesus?
- Note the emphasis on:
    ◊ the presence of the Holy Spirit with Jesus;
    ◊ Jesus is the one who is anointed and sent by God.
- What areas of ministry and service are mentioned in this Scripture?
- How do we as a church and as individuals participate in these ministries?

Wrapping Up

Closing Activity

Give each participant a three-by-five card.

Remind the group of the three questions considered during this session:

- Who do you say Jesus is…every day?
- Who do you say Jesus is now?
- What difference does your answer make in your life?

Instruct participants to:

- select a question they want to focus on during the week;
- write the question on the three-by-five card; and
- put the card in a place they will see it frequently during the week.

Closing Prayer

Close your time together with the following prayer or offer one of your own.

Loving God, open my heart and my mind so that I may grow in my understanding of who you are and who you call me to be, in the name of your Son, Jesus Christ. Amen.

SESSION 2

Why Are You Afraid?

Planning the Session

Session Goals

Through conversation, activities, and reflection, participants will:

- Consider these questions:
  ◊ What makes me afraid?
  ◊ When am I afraid?
  ◊ Where am I afraid?
  ◊ Of whom am I afraid?
- Explore in depth their response to Jesus's question:
  "Why are you afraid?"
- Identify ways to overcome fear.

Biblical Foundation

Matthew 8:23-27

Before the Session

- Set up a table in the room with nametags and markers, Bibles, and extra copies of *Questions Jesus Asked* if any of these will be needed. Also set out the sign-in and attendance sheet so participants can mark their attendance and newcomers can add their contact information.
- On a whiteboard, chalkboard, or large piece of chart paper. draw three vertical lines to make four columns. Write these headings in the columns: *what, when, where, who.*
- Read the Optional Activity and decide if you want to include it in your lesson plan.

Getting Started

Introductions

Greet participants as they arrive. Invite each to make a nametag and pick up a Bible and/or copy of *Questions Jesus Asked* if needed.

Welcome participants. If there are newcomers, allow a short time for introductions.

Housekeeping

- Refer to the list in session 1 and share any information that needs to be repeated.
- Remind participants of the covenant to respect confidentiality within the group.

Leading into the Study

Call attention to the board or chart paper with the four headings: *what, when, where, who.*

Say:

We may be afraid in a variety of situations and circumstances. These may include a fear of heights, a fear of public speaking, and a fear of having surgery. As you respond to these questions, consider all of the situations and circumstances that may cause you to feel afraid.

Ask these questions, one at a time, and record responses on the board or chart paper below the appropriate heading.

- What makes you afraid?
- When are you afraid?
- Where are you afraid?
- Of whom are you afraid?

Opening Prayer

Lead the group in the following prayer or one of your own.

Loving God, you know there are times when we feel afraid. There are times when we, like the disciples, want to cry out, "Lord, rescue us! We're going to drown!" We remember that many times in Scripture you tell us not to be afraid. You assure us of your faithful mercy and presence. Thank you for this time of fellowship and Bible study. Open our hearts and minds to receive your word for us as we examine the question Jesus asked the disciples, "Why are you afraid?" In the name of your Son, Jesus, we pray. Amen.

Learning Together

Video Study and Discussion

Invite the group to consider these three questions as they view the video:

- Are you able to sleep like Jesus?
- How does the image of a powerful storm help you describe your experiences of challenging and frightening situations?
- When have you experienced a peace that passed your understanding?
- What does this story teach us about God? (*God is powerful. God is always present with us.*)

Following the video, invite volunteers to share their responses to the questions above.

Bible Study and Discussion: Matthew 8:23-27

Read or invite a volunteer to read the Biblical Foundation Scripture, Matthew 8:23-27. Then read or invite volunteers to read this story as recorded in Mark 4:35-41 and Luke 8:22-25.

Explain that people in biblical times viewed the sea as a frightening place because:

- they believed it was the entrance to the underworld; and
- it was home to sea monsters, for example, Leviathan.

Highlight de Vega's comment from the opening section of chapter 2, "the sea is a symbol of chaos and death. It's a force that inspires fear." **Say:**

With this in mind, we can understand this description of God's heavenly kingdom in the Book of Revelation: "Then I saw a new heaven and a new earth, for the former heaven and the former earth had passed away, and the sea was no more" (Revelation 21:1).

Read again the verses that describe the storm, printed below from the Common English Bible. Before you read, **ask:** "What descriptive words about the storm the disciples experienced stand out for you?" (You may want to write these on a board or chart paper during the discussion.)

- "A huge storm arose on the lake so that waves were sloshing over the boat" (Matthew 8:24).
- "Gale-force winds arose, and waves crashed against the boat so that the boat was swamped" (Mark 4:37).
- "Gale-force winds swept down on the lake. The boat was filling up with water and they were in danger" (Luke 8:23).

Invite participants in your group with different versions of the Bible to read these verses for comparison. **Ask:**

- When have your experiences of fear caused you to feel as if you were in a storm?

Book Study and Discussion

Call attention to deVega's observation that in the Gospels of Mark and Luke, Jesus calms the storm before he speaks to his disciples (Mark 4:39; Luke 8:24). In contrast, in the Gospel of Matthew, Jesus speaks to the disciples before he calms the storm (Matthew 8:26).

Note that the Gospel of Matthew reports a second story of Jesus calming the sea (Matthew 14:22-33). In this story Peter walked toward Jesus, then became frightened and began to sink. Jesus "grabbed him" and walked with him through the storm to the boat (v. 31). When they were safely in the boat, "the wind settled down" (v. 32).

Ask:

- When have you heard the Lord speaking to you before calming the storm that frightened you?
- When have you experienced the Lord calming the storm first, and then speaking to you?

Invite participants to refer to the section "Asking and Hearing Questions Differently" during the discussion of the following questions.

Remind the group of the question Jesus asked his disciples (Matthew 8:26), "Why are you afraid, you people of weak faith?" **Ask:**

- What tone of voice do you imagine Jesus using when he asked this question of the disciples?
- What is the difference between asking a question as a means of interrogation and asking a question out of curiosity?
- What difference does it make for you to hear Jesus ask this question more out of curiosity than of judgment? (Reflection question from end of chapter 2 in *Questions Jesus Asked*)

Highlight this quote from *Questions Jesus Asked*:

Maybe Jesus is neither ignoring the disciples' fear nor rebuking them for it, but introducing a way to conquer their fear through the simple act of asking a question with disarming curiosity.

"Why *are* you afraid? What is it that scares you? What do you think is the limit of your faith right now?"

...Imagine Jesus asking you these questions...to invite you to explore the source of that fear, to test its validity, and to learn to rely on what is true instead of on the falsehoods that fear would have you believe.

Invite discussion of the questions asked in the quote above. Invite participants to consider the questions from the viewpoint of curiosity.

- Why are you afraid?
- What is it that scares you?
- What do you think is the limit of your faith right now?

Call attention to the acronym for FEAR—False Evidence Appearing Real. **Ask:**

- To what degree do you believe your fears are grounded in truth? (paraphrased Reflection question from the end of chapter 2)

Summarize or invite a volunteer to summarize the experience of John Wesley in the section "A Lesson from John Wesley." Then **ask:**

- What did the Moravian Christians do during the storm at sea that allowed them to remain calm? (*Sing and serve*)

- How do these activities bring us peace during the frightening times in our lives? (*Singing comforts us. Serving comforts others and moves our focus from our own safety to ways we can help.*)

Invite a volunteer to read Philippians 4:4-7. **Ask:**

- What does the apostle Paul encourage Christians to do to know "the peace of God that exceeds all understanding"? (You may want to list these on a board or chart paper.)
- How do these instructions in Philippians 4:4-7 help you experience God's peace? How does the knowledge that God is always with you give you peace during frightening, challenging, and difficult times?

Invite participants to turn to the section "What Kind of Man Is This?" Highlight this quote: "[Jesus] speaks to the storm *within* us, to show us how to combat our stormy fears through the simple act of asking it questions."

Invite discussion of the questions in the section "What Kind of Man Is This?" printed below:

- Where does your fear come from?
- Do you believe that your fear is the truth?
- What is the worst that could happen?
- What would you be able to do if you weren't afraid?

Then **ask:**

- When you experience fear, how is it helpful to you to ask the questions above?
- How do you answer the disciples' question, "What sort of man is this, that even the winds and the sea obey him?" (Matthew 8:27 NRSVUE; see also Luke 8:25).

Optional Activity: Songs, Scriptures, and Poems That Calm Our Fears

Call attention to the poems and songs mentioned in chapter 2 that can help calm our fears. **Ask:**

- What songs, Scriptures, and poems calm your fears and assure you of God's presence when you are frightened?

Wrapping Up

Closing Activity

Read the closing sentences of chapter 2:

God does not leave us to be overcome by our fears. God comes to us through Jesus Christ, conquering the waves of our apprehensions, stilling the storms of uncertainty. In Jesus God calls us to trust and surrender ourselves to the loving and powerful arms of God.

That is the future that God desires for you. It is a life that is neither free from fear nor dictated by it. It's a life in which you engage your fear and allow God to transform it to make you stronger and more faithful.

Closing Prayer

Close your time together with the following prayer or offer one of your own.

Loving God, thank you for your continuing presence and faithfulness. Let us remember that you are always with us. When we are afraid, help us remember to ask questions about our fear and to look at the reasons we feel afraid. Guide us as we discern answers to our questions. Help us to comfort others when they are afraid, as you provide comfort for us in frightening times. In the name of your Son, Jesus, we pray. Amen.

SESSION 3

Why Are You Anxious?

Planning the Session

Session Goals

Through conversation, activities, and reflection, participants will:

- Explore the meaning of these key ideas in the Biblical Foundation Scripture:
  ◊ "Stop worrying"
  ◊ "desire his kingdom"
  ◊ "Who among you by worrying can add a single moment to your life?"
- Discover how practicing spiritual disciplines helps calm our worrying, specifically the disciplines of:
  ◊ breath prayers
  ◊ the Daily Examen
  ◊ thankfulness

Biblical Foundation

Luke 12:25-31

Before the Session

- Set up a table in the room with nametags and markers, Bibles, and extra copies of *Questions Jesus Asked* if any of these will be needed. Also set out the sign-in and attendance sheet so participants can mark their attendance and newcomers can add their contact information.

- Have a whiteboard and markers, a chalkboard and chalk, or an easel and markers available for the "Leading into the Study" discussion.
- Read the Optional Activity and decide if you want to include "Create Your Own Breath Prayers" in your lesson plan.

Getting Started

Introductions

Greet participants as they arrive. Invite each to make a nametag and pick up a Bible and/or copy of *Questions Jesus Asked* if needed.

Welcome participants. If there are newcomers, allow a short time for introductions.

Housekeeping

- Refer to the list in session 1 and share any information that needs to be repeated.
- Remind participants of the covenant to respect confidentiality within the group.

Leading into the Study

Invite discussion of the following questions. During the discussion, record responses on a board or chart paper. **Ask:**

- When do you say thank you to God for your blessings? (Encourage participants to include times when they are alone and times when they offer thanks to God with others.)
- For what blessing(s) do you most frequently offer thanks?

Opening Prayer

Loving God, we hear the words of Jesus telling us, "Stop worrying." We hear the words of Jesus assuring us that you know what we need and you will provide for us. Yet, sometimes we worry anyway. We worry about what will happen. We worry about what we should do or should not do. We worry about the people we love. Help us, O God. Help us learn to take time to breathe and be truly aware of your presence. Help us remember the many blessings you offer us. Calm our anxious hearts. In the name of your Son, Jesus, we pray. Amen.

Learning Together

Video Study and Discussion (optional)

Before viewing the video, highlight two of Magrey de Vega's key points:

1. Worry is a part of life;
2. We need to work together as a society to remove the stigma related to anxiety and other mental health concerns.

Instruct participants to listen for the four things we may say to our worry.

After viewing the video **ask:**

- Why does Jesus ask his disciples this question about worrying? (*So we will not allow worry to paralyze us.*)
- What are the four things de Vega suggests we may say to our worry?
- How does worry help us grow?

Following the video, invite volunteers to share their responses to the questions above.

Bible Study and Discussion

Invite a volunteer to read the Biblical Foundation Scripture, Luke 12:25-31.

Invite discussion of the following key ideas from the Scripture.

From verse 29: "Stop worrying." **Ask:**

- Why does Jesus tell us, "Stop worrying"?
- To what extent do you think the worries of people who lived in Jesus's time are the same and/or different from the worries we have today? (See opening paragraphs of chapter 3 in *Questions Jesus Asked.*)

From verses 29 and 31: "Don't chase after what you will eat and what you will drink....Instead, desire his kingdom." **Ask:**

- What does it mean to you to desire God's kingdom?

Ask:

- How do you think the regular practice of the Daily Examen might lead you to focus more on God's kingdom (Luke 12:31) and worry less?

Call attention to John Wesley's "personal gratitude inventory," which is a practice similar in purpose to the Daily Examen. Invite discussion of John Wesley's three questions.

Question 1: "Have I allotted some time for thanking God for the blessings of the past week?"

Ask:

- How will being intentional about setting aside time to express gratitude to God help you grow in faith and worry less?

Question 2: "Have I, in order to be the more sensible of them, seriously and deliberately considered the several circumstances that attended them?"

Note de Vega's rewording of this question: "Is it possible that God was blessing me even when I was at my lowest point this week? Is it possible that even when I was facing significant challenges, God was in fact still there to give me strength?" **Ask:**

- Are you mindful of God's blessings even in the midst of challenges, hardship, and grief?
- If so, how does this mindfulness alleviate or lessen your worry?

Question 3: "Have I considered each of them as an obligation to greater love, and consequently, to stricter holiness?"

Note de Vega's rewording of this question: "In what way is God blessing me, even through the darkness and toughness of life, to be a blessing for someone else?" **Ask:**

- How does gratitude for God's blessings instill in you the desire to reach out to serve others so God can bless others through you?

Optional Activity: Create Your Own Breath Prayers

Note: Some of this material in this Optional Activity is from Jane E. Vennard and Stephen D. Bryant, *The Way of Prayer Participants Book* (Nashville: Upper Room Books, 2007), p. 41.

Explain:

- Breath prayers help us "express our deepest needs" to God.
- Usually "breath prayers are six to eight syllables and fit easily into one inhale and exhale."

Share two examples of breath prayers:

- "Let me know your peace, O God."
- "Jesus, let me feel your love."

Invite participants to sit comfortably and close their eyes. Lead them in each of these breath prayers: "Let me know your peace, O God" and "Jesus, let me feel your love." Repeat the first prayer three times in the slow rhythm of an inhale and an exhale. Then do the same with the second prayer.

When you have finished, invite the group to open their eyes. Encourage the group to use one of these breath prayers in the coming week, or to make their own by combining a name for God with a simple, short request.

Wrapping Up

Closing Activity

Read the first paragraph in the section of chapter 3 titled "Combating Anxiety with Action": "Ultimately, our free will is a gift from God, and it can be useful in combating anxiety. We are not helpless in any situation. God has empowered us to be resistant, proactive, and prepared. Action can be a part of anxiety's antidote."

Ask these "Questions for Reflection" from the end of chapter 3:

- "What actions can you take to combat your worries?"
- "How will you pay more attention to things you can be grateful for?"

Call attention to deVega's idea of a "private gratitude inventory" that he describes in the section titled "Keeping Track of Gratitude." Encourage participants to consider keeping such an inventory. This inventory may be kept in a journal, a notebook, or in digital form.

Closing Prayer

Close your time together with the following prayer or offer one of your own.

Loving and ever-present God, you tell us to "stop worrying." Sometimes that seems like an impossible instruction to follow because there seem to be so many things to worry about. Yet we know you love us. We know you will always care for us. Help us to desire your kingdom more than anything else. Help us to be mindful of your presence and blessings every day. Thank you for the ways you are present with us, guiding us and loving us. Use us to bless others and to help others be mindful of your presence so they, too, may worry less and desire your kingdom more; in the name of your Son, Jesus Christ. Amen.

SESSION 4

What Do You Live For?

Planning the Session

Session Goals

Through conversation, activities, and reflection, participants will:

- discern what it means to "save" and "lose" one's life in the context of following Jesus;
- explore spiritual practices that help us grow as faithful followers of Jesus; and
- consider their response to the question asked in the session title: "What Do You Live For?"

Biblical Foundation

Mark 8:34-38

Before the Session

- Set up a table in the room with nametags and markers, Bibles, and extra copies of *Questions Jesus Asked* if any of these will be needed. Also set out the sign-in and attendance sheet so participants can mark their attendance and newcomers can add their contact information.
- Write the words *save* and *lose* on a board or large piece of paper. This is for the Bible Study and Discussion.
- Read the Optional Activity and decide if you want to include the discussion in your lesson plan.

Getting Started

Introductions

Greet participants as they arrive. Invite each to make a nametag and pick up a Bible and/or copy of *Questions Jesus Asked* if needed.

Welcome participants. If there are newcomers, allow a short time for introductions.

Housekeeping

- Refer to the list in session 1 and share any information that needs to be repeated.
- Remind participants of the covenant to respect confidentiality within the group.

Leading into the Study

Say: The question Jesus asked that we will focus on in this session is "Why would people gain the whole world but lose their lives?" In the opening section of chapter 4, deVega asks several questions that relate to this question. They are:

- What are you really living for?
- What good will it do you if you spend your life pursuing things that ultimately do not matter, rather than discovering the true life God desires for you?
- What are you worshipping?
- What are you becoming?

Instruct participants to keep these questions in mind during the session. Let them know you will revisit these questions and offer time for discussion at the end of the session.

Opening Prayer

Loving God, thank you for this time of fellowship and Bible study. Open our minds to understand what you are saying to us through this Scripture. Open our hearts to receive your holy Word. Give us courage to follow Jesus in a world that tempts us to do otherwise. In the name of your Son, Jesus, we pray. Amen.

Learning Together

Video Study and Discussion

Invite the group to consider these questions as they view the video:

- What labels do you use to identify yourself?
- How does Jesus desire that we see ourselves?
- How has Jesus reversed and/or transformed your expectations and priorities?
- What reversals and transformations are continuing to take place in your life though Christ?
- What does it mean to you to take up the cross by which Jesus delivered/saved you and follow him?

Following the video, invite volunteers to share their responses to the questions above.

Bible Study and Discussion

Invite a volunteer to read the Biblical Foundation Scripture, Mark 8:34-38.

Call attention to the words *lose* and *save* on the board or chart paper.

Explain that early Christians lived in a time of persecution and martyrdom for some. This is the context in which they would have read and interpreted Mark's gospel.

Read verse 35 again. Note that the words *save* and *lose* are each used twice in this verse. **Ask:**

- What does it mean to you to save your life in the world? (Responses may center around *holding on to what the world values,* for example *social standing or career advancement, even if it means losing our faithful relationship with the Lord.*)
- What do we lose when we save our lives according to the world's values? (For example, *we lose the joy, peace, and hope that come from a relationship with the Lord.*)
- What does it mean to you to lose your life for the sake of Jesus and the good news? (Responses may center around the idea of *giving up self-centered desires and living a God-centered life.*)

- How do we save our lives when we choose to lose them for Jesus and the gospel? (Responses may center around the ideas of *saving the life God calls us to live, saving our lives from the consequences of sin, receiving the gift of salvation and inheriting eternal life.*)

Read verse 38 again. Then read this quote (*The CEB Study Bible* footnote, p. 84 NT). "Jesus' call for self-sacrifice would have been humiliating to ancient hearers, since he's urging voluntary weakness in a culture that avoids it."

Ask:

- What sacrifices do we make as followers of Jesus? (Examples of things we may sacrifice include: *time for a vacation to participate in a mission trip; financial resources to help others; a high-paying job for a lower-paying job that fits our Christian lifestyle better.* Encourage participants to think about the choices they make that put meeting the needs of others over personal desires.)
- When have you said no to yourself? (verse 34) (This question is similar to the previous question and offers another way to think about sacrifice.)
- How might we be ridiculed or criticized by the world for making these sacrifices?
- How have non-believers tried to make you feel ashamed of your choices when you follow Jesus?

Book Study and Discussion

Read Mark 8:36 from the CEB and the NRSVUE:

- "Why would people gain the whole world but lose their lives?" (CEB)
- "For what will it profit them to gain the whole world and forfeit their life?" (NRSVUE).

Share these key points:

- The Gospel of Mark was written in Greek.
- The Greek word for life is *psyche*, which may be translated "life," "mind," or "soul."

Ask:

* What gifts from God does the gift of life encompass?
  (Gifts mentioned in *Questions Jesus Asked* include: *our identity, passion, personality, emotions, intellect, and abilities.*)

Read the two-part definition of *soul* in the section "Gaining Your Soul": "Our souls are the source of our lives that draw us into the Source of All Life."

Read the quote from Saint Augustine in *Questions Jesus Asks*: "You have made us and drawn us to yourself, and our heart is unquiet until it rests in you."

Call attention to the connection between the two-part definition of *soul* and the feelings expressed by Augustine:

Two-Part Definition	*Saint Augustine*
"Our souls are the source of our lives"	"you have made us"
"Our souls…draw us into the Source of All Life."	"you have…drawn us to yourself"

Highlight the last part of Augustine's statement, "our heart is unquiet until it rests in you."

Note that the psalmist expressed similar feelings. Read Psalm 42:1-2.

Just like a deer that craves streams of water,
  my whole being craves you, God.
My whole being thirsts for God, for the living God.
  When will I come and see God's face?

Ask:

* When have you experienced the yearning or craving to feel closer to God?
* What helps you satisfy this longing for God?
* When has your soul felt crushed, and when has it felt lifted?
  (Reflection question from the end of chapter 4)

Let the discussion of the questions on the previous page lead into a conversation about the spiritual practices. Introduce the conversation by saying:

- The spiritual practices provide a way for us to:
  ◊ satisfy our longing for God;
  ◊ listen for God speaking in our daily life; and
  ◊ grow in spiritual maturity.

- In the previous session we explored the spiritual practices of:
  ◊ breath prayers;
  ◊ the Daily Examen; and
  ◊ gratitude.

- Chapter 4 invites us to explore these spiritual practices:
  ◊ worship;
  ◊ small groups;
  ◊ service;
  ◊ financial giving;
  ◊ Bible study;
  ◊ inviting others; and
  ◊ prayer

Ask:

- What spiritual disciplines do you practice?
- Which spiritual practices are the most meaningful or helpful to you?
- What spiritual disciplines would you like to practice more or learn more about?
- What, if anything, prevents you from engaging the spiritual practices?
- What does the acronym G.R.I.P. stand for?

Invite participants to turn to the sections titled:

- "Give Generously"
- "Read the Scriptures"
- "Invite Others to Faith in Jesus"
- "Pray Regularly"

Discuss each section separately using this question as a guide:

- What stands out for you about this spiritual practice?

Optional Activity: Mark 8:34

You may want to spend more time exploring the meaning of Mark 8:34, the first verse of the Biblical Foundation Scripture.

Read the verse: "All who want to come after me must say no to themselves, take up their cross, and follow me." **Ask:**

- What is the significance of the word *want*?

Key points to add to the conversation include the following:

- ◊ God created us to have free will (session 3).
- ◊ Taking up our cross and following Jesus is a choice.
- ◊ We have the freedom to say no to ourselves or no to Jesus.
- ◊ Jesus chose to take up his cross; he did so willingly.

- Why did Jesus want to take up his cross?

Ideas include:

- ◊ Jesus wanted to fulfill God's call and purpose for his life.
- ◊ Jesus was willing to sacrifice his life for the good of others and for the salvation of all humankind.
- ◊ Why would we choose to take up our cross?
- ◊ Responses may include:
- ◊ To fulfill God's call for our lives.
- ◊ To serve others.

Summarize the story in the opening section about the conversation between William Willimon and a parent about a student. The student said no to the world and yes to Jesus. She chose to take up the "cross" of serving others in an impoverished country. **Ask:**

- What "cross" (or crosses) have you felt called by God to take up?
- What "cross" (or crosses) have you chosen to accept and take up?

Wrapping Up

Closing Activity

Invite discussion of the questions de Vega asked in the opening section of chapter 4:

- What are you really living for?
- What good will it do you if you spend your life pursuing things that ultimately do not matter, rather than discovering the true life God desires for you?
- What are you worshipping?
- What are you becoming?

Closing Prayer

Close your time together with the following prayer or offer one of your own.

Loving and ever-present God, we want to follow Jesus. We look to you for wisdom as we discern your call for our lives. We look to you for courage as we say no to the life the world offers us and yes to the life you offer us. In the name of your Son, Jesus Christ, we pray. Amen.

SESSION 5

Whom Will You Love?

Planning the Session

Session Goals

Through conversation, activities, and reflection, participants will:

- discover the way Jesus's original audience understood his teachings in this Scripture passage;
- explore in depth what it means to love our enemies; and
- affirm the power of forgiveness.

Biblical Foundation

Luke 6:27-36

Before the Session

- Set up a table in the room with nametags and markers, Bibles, and extra copies of *Questions Jesus Asked* if any of these will be needed. Also set out the sign-in and attendance sheet so participants can mark their attendance and newcomers can add their contact information.
- Read the Optional Activity. If you want to include it in your lesson plan, either (1) write the beginning proverb phrases on a board or chart paper, or (2) make copies of the phrases on printer paper to distribute to participants. Also have paper and pencils or pens available.

Getting Started

Introductions

Greet participants as they arrive. Invite each to make a nametag and pick up a Bible and/or copy of *Questions Jesus Asked* if needed.

Welcome participants. If there are newcomers, allow a short time for introductions.

Housekeeping

- Refer to the list in session 1 and share any information that needs to be repeated.
- Remind participants of the covenant to respect confidentiality within the group.

Leading into the Study

Lead a discussion centered around the title for this session, "Whom Will You Love?" **Ask:**

- Whom do you love? Who are the people that first come to mind when you hear this question?
- Who do you find it easy to love?
- Why is it easy to love them?
- Who do you find it hard to love?
- What makes it difficult to love them?

Opening Prayer

Open with the following prayer or one of your own.

Holy and merciful God, you are love. You created us out of love. You gave your Son, Jesus Christ, for our salvation because you love us. We remember the Scripture that tells us we love because you loved us first [see 1 John 4:19]. Thank you for this time of fellowship and Bible study. Open our hearts as we learn more together about what it means to truly live as your loving and compassionate people. In the name of your Son, Jesus, we pray. Amen.

Learning Together

Video Study and Discussion

Invite the group to consider these three questions as they view the video:

- Why is it important to balance truth and love in our relationships with others?

49

- Why is this sometimes difficult?
- What experience led John Wesley to have a "passion for the truth"? (*Aldersgate Street*)
- What experience led John Wesley to have a "compassion for people"? (*preaching throughout England*)
- How do you balance a passion for the truth and compassion for people in your own life?

Following the video, invite volunteers to share their responses to the questions above.

Bible Study and Discussion

This Bible Study and Discussion will look at three different, yet related, passages of Scripture: Luke 6:27-31, Matthew 5:38-42, and Exodus 21:23-25.

Read or invite a volunteer to read Luke 6:27-31 from the Biblical Foundation Scripture.

Invite another volunteer to read the similar passage from Matthew's gospel, Matthew 5:38-42.

Then read Exodus 21:23-25 printed here: "If there is further injury, then you will give a life for a life, an eye for an eye, a tooth for a tooth, a hand for a hand, a foot for a foot, a burn for a burn, a bruise for a bruise, a wound for a wound."

Note that on the surface this passage from Exodus seems to give permission for revenge or retaliation. Yet, this instruction had another purpose. One theologian writes, "The instruction puts a limit on how much revenge can be taken in response to a death or injury....this instruction also doesn't allow simple payment of money as a sufficient penalty for taking a life or a limb from another human being" (*The CEB Study Bible*, footnote, p. 119 OT).

Invite participants to refer to these sections of *Questions Jesus Asked* during the discussion of the following questions.

- "Turn the Other Cheek"
- "Give Away Your Shirt"
- "Walk the Extra Mile"

Read these instructions from Luke and Matthew:

- "If someone slaps you on the cheek, offer the other one as well" (Luke 6:29).
- "If people slap you on your right cheek, you must turn the left cheek to them as well" (Matthew 5:39).

Ask:

- How have you usually interpreted these verses of Scripture?
- How would the people in Jesus's day have interpreted the meaning of turning the other cheek? (*It was a way of maintaining one's dignity and self-respect.* See the section "Turn the Other Cheek" in *Questions Jesus Asked.*)
- How do you respond to humiliation and maintain your dignity?
- Who are people in our society who are humiliated and degraded by individuals or systems? (Examples are: *victims of spousal abuse, child abuse, or prejudice against different individuals or groups of people.*)
- How are we as individuals, churches, and communities reaching out to defend the dignity of all God's people?

Read these verses from Luke and Matthew:

- "If someone takes your coat, don't withhold your shirt either" (Luke 6:29).
- "When they wish to haul you to court and take your shirt, let them have your coat too" (Matthew 5:40).

Ask:

- How have you usually interpreted these verses of Scripture?
- How would the people in Jesus's day have interpreted the meaning of not withholding your shirt? (*This was a nonviolent way to respond to oppression.* See the section "Give Away Your Shirt.")
- When have you been the victim of oppression?
- How did you respond?
- Who are individuals and groups, both local and global, experiencing oppression?

- How are we as individuals, churches, and communities reaching out on behalf of oppressed people?

Read Matthew 5:41. (The Gospel of Luke does not include a corresponding verse.): "When they force you to go one mile, go with them two." **Ask:**

- How have you usually interpreted this verse of Scripture?
- How would the people in Jesus's day have interpreted the meaning of going an extra mile? (*This was a nonviolent way to expose injustice and inequities.* See the section "Walk the Extra Mile.")
- When have you been the victim of injustice or been treated as if you were not equal to others?
- How did you respond?
- What examples of inequality exist in our communities and around the world today? (*Consider inequalities based on gender, sexuality, ethnicity, religious preference, and economic status, for example.*)
- How are we as individuals, churches, and communities working to alleviate these inequalities?

Close this Bible Study and Discussion by noting that bringing an end to situations of humiliation, oppression, injustice, and inequity can seem overwhelming. We make progress one step at a time. Encourage participants to become involved in their local church ministries and community outreach programs that address these issues. Consult websites—for example, The United Methodist General Board of Global Ministries and UMCOR—to learn about ways The United Methodist Church is at work addressing these issues around the world.

Book Study and Discussion

Read Luke 6:31:

- "Treat people in the same way that you want them to treat you." (CEB)
- "Do to others as you would have them do to you." (NRSVUE and NIV)

Call attention to deVega's statement that all major religions include an expression of the Golden Rule. Read the examples of these provided in the opening section of chapter 5.

Highlight de Vega's point that this instruction of Jesus is easy to understand but not easy to apply. **Ask:**

- How might we misinterpret the meaning of the Golden Rule? (Invite participants to refer to the opening section of chapter 5 as they respond.)
- What is required if we are to obey the Golden Rule in a way that is effective and beneficial? (*Empathy*)
- Invite a volunteer to read the definition and insights about empathy at the end of the opening section of chapter 5.

Read the Biblical Foundation Scripture, Luke 6:27-36. (This includes the verses that were discussed in the Bible Study and Discussion segment.) **Ask:**

- Who is your enemy?
- How do you determine if someone or some group is an enemy?
- Why is it difficult for us to love an enemy?

Invite a volunteer to summarize or read the story of Takunda Mavima in the section "The Power of Forgiveness."

Invite another volunteer to summarize or read the story about the Sikh congregation. **Ask:**

- What are your thoughts about these stories?
- What are the possible long-lasting results and benefits of forgiveness for:
  ◊ the victims?
  ◊ the perpetrators?
  ◊ the bystanders and people who heard the stories?
- When have you received forgiveness from someone you considered an enemy?
- How did this forgiveness impact your relationship with this person or group?
- How did this forgiveness impact your life?
- When have you forgiven someone who wronged you or caused you harm?
- What was this experience like for you?

- How did the relationship change because of your forgiveness?
- What is the relationship between empathy and forgiveness? (Remind the group that "empathy is our capacity to see the world and the situation through the eyes and perspective of another person," p. 97)

Optional Activity: If your enemies...

Before the session write these beginning phrases on a board or chart paper; then turn or cover the board or chart paper so participants will not be able to read the phrases before you introduce the activity. You may choose instead to make copies on printer paper to distribute to each participant at the time you introduce the discussion.

- If your enemies say hurtful things to you,...
- If your enemies vandalize your property,...
- If your enemies are oppressing your neighbor,...
- If your enemies are living in your neighborhood,...

Introduce the activity by reading Proverbs 25:21.

If your enemies are starving, feed them some bread;
> *if they are thirsty, give them water to drink.*

Create small groups of two to four people. Let the small groups know how much time is available for this activity (five minutes is suggested). Distribute paper and pencils or pens to each small group.

If you printed the proverb beginning phrases, distribute them now. If you wrote the beginning phrases on a board or chart paper, display them now.

Offer these instructions:

- Complete these proverbs.
- Preface each proverb with Jesus's teaching "Love your enemies" (Luke 6:27).

Read this example:

- "Love your enemies. If your enemies are starving, feed them some bread."

At the end of the time for the activity, call the groups back together.

Read each proverb, one at a time, prefacing each proverb with "Love your enemies."

Invite each group to share how they completed that proverb. Groups may share more than one example.

If a group completes a proverb with "forgive them," accept the response and then ask what might be involved in that process of forgiveness.

When you complete the activity, **ask:**

- What was it like for you to complete these proverbs?
- What came easy for you?
- What made it difficult?

Wrapping Up

Closing Activity

Offer time for quiet reflection of these questions. **Ask:**

- Who do you need to forgive?
- Is it easy or difficult for you to forgive that person or group of people?
- How will empathy for each person help you forgive him or her?

These are personal questions, and participants may prefer to keep their responses private. If anyone does want to share, offer time for the participant to do so.

Closing Prayer

Close your time together with the following prayer or offer one of your own.

Loving and ever-present God, thank you for loving us. We confess that it is not always easy for us to love others, especially those we consider to be our enemies. Help us to have empathy for others. Open our hearts to be forgiving, remembering that you have forgiven us; in the name of your Son, Jesus Christ. Amen.

SESSION 6

What Are You Looking For?

Planning the Session

Session Goals

Through conversation, activities, and reflection, participants will:

- consider the question in the session title, "What are you looking for?"
- discern, or begin the process of discerning God's purpose for their lives
- review and reflect on the six questions of Jesus highlighted in *Questions Jesus Asked*. (This goal relates to the Optional Activity.)

Biblical Foundation

John 1:35-38

Before the Session

- Set up a table in the room with nametags and markers, Bibles, and extra copies of *Questions Jesus Asked* if any of these will be needed. Also set out the sign-in and attendance sheet so participants can mark their attendance and newcomers can add their contact information.
- Write the question, "What are you looking for?" at the top of a board or piece of chart paper. Leave room below to record group responses.
- Have paper and pencils or pens available for use during the Book Study and Discussion and the Optional Activity.
- Read the Optional Activity and decide if you want to include it in your lesson plan.

Getting Started

Introductions

Greet participants as they arrive. Invite each to make a nametag and pick up a Bible and/or copy of *Questions Jesus Asked* if needed.

Welcome participants. If there are newcomers, allow a short time for introductions.

Housekeeping

- Refer to the list in session 1 and share any information that needs to be repeated.
- Remind participants of the covenant to respect confidentiality within the group.

Leading into the Study

Call attention to the board or paper with the heading "What are you looking for?"

Instruct participants to call out short answers to the question below. Write the responses under the heading. Keep the responses for reference later in the session. **Ask:**

- How do you answer Jesus's question, "What are you looking for?"

Opening Prayer

Open with the following prayer or one of your own.

Holy and loving God, you ask us questions that invite us to seriously consider our faith and our relationship with you. You ask us questions that draw us closer to you and the life you desire for us. We thank you for the questions. We pray for wisdom as we seek the answers. We pray for courage as we seek to live the lives to which you call us. Thank you for this time of study and for the fellowship with your followers. Help us to be faithful disciples. In the name of your Son, Jesus, we pray. Amen.

Learning Together

Video Study and Discussion (optional)

Invite the group to consider these four questions as they view the video:

- Why is it important to go deeper into our spiritual life?

The following three questions relate to de Vega's three practical ways to go deeper into the spiritual life.

- What spiritual friends have helped you grow deeper in your faith in Christ?
- What distractions can you take out of your life so you may spend more time engaged in spiritual practices that will help you go deeper in your faith?
- How has God been at work in your life orchestrating events and providing resources to help you go deeper?

Following the video, invite volunteers to share their responses to the questions above.

Bible Study and Discussion

Read the story of John the Baptist as recorded in John 1:19-34. This precedes the Biblical Foundation Scripture for this session.

Then invite a volunteer to read the Biblical Foundation Scripture, John 1:35-38.

Explain that we are told in verse 40 that one of the disciples "was Andrew, the brother of Simon Peter." **Ask:**

- When the two disciples left John to follow Jesus, why was Jesus's question, "What are you looking for?" so important?
- When the disciples asked Jesus, "Where are you staying?" what were they really asking? (Call attention to the section "Where Are You Staying?" where de Vega writes, "They were asking how they might *abide* with him. How they might draw close to him, how they might follow him, and most important, whether Jesus could provide the one thing they were craving and longing for: stability.")
- How does the disciples' question "Where are you staying?" reveal their answer to the question Jesus asked them, "What are you looking for?" (The disciples were looking for the "stability," "grounding," and "foundation" that Jesus could offer them. These desires are reflected in the word *staying*, which in this context has the deeper meaning of "abiding.")

**To the leader: Participants may be familiar with the story of Jesus calling Peter and Andrew to be his disciples while they were fishing and ask why the difference in the Gospel of John. Explain that the story of Jesus calling Peter and Andrew while they were fishing is recorded in the three Synoptic Gospels: Matthew 4:18-20; Mark 1:16-18; and Luke 5:1-11. The writers of these Gospels had access to some of the same source documents. There are similarities in content and style; hence, the name "Synoptic Gospels." John's Gospel differs in content in places. For example, the stories of Jesus talking with the woman at the well in Samaria and Jesus washing his disciples' feet at the Last Supper are only recorded in John. John also has a different writing style.

Book Study and Discussion

Review the illustration of the circles that represent theology and significant events, using the section "The Two Circles Revisited" as a guide.

Lead the group in identifying key events and turning points in de Vega's story of growing in faith, using the following questions as a guide. Invite participants to refer to the sections "Living the Questions" and "Discovering the Story Within My Story" during the discussion. **Ask:**

- What kind of Christian upbringing did de Vega experience as a child and teenager?
- What happened when de Vega went to college?
- What tension was de Vega trying to resolve in college? (*the tension between significant life events and theology, the two circles*)
- With which biblical character did de Vega identify? (*Joseph*)
- How did he find his story in Joseph's story?
- What happened in de Vega's friendship with his roommate?
- How did this advice from one of de Vega's former Sunday school teachers influence his life? "(Magrey, instead of seeing yourself as the only one on that campus, how about seeing yourself as just the first one?")
- What happened next?

Invite participants to move into small groups of two to four people for the discussion of the following questions. Ask the questions one at a time, offer a few minutes for the small groups to discuss, and then invite each group to share one or two examples or insights before asking the next question.

Ask:

- What experiences during your childhood and teenage years helped form your first understandings of the Christian faith?
- When did you experience these early understandings being affirmed and/or challenged as you grew older?
- What key events in your life have influenced or impacted your faith?
- Who have been mentors for you during your journey of faith?

Ask the following two questions together:

- With which biblical character do you most identify?
- Where do you see your story in that person's story?

Then **ask:**

- What does the resurrection of Jesus mean to you?

Call the small groups back together. Highlight de Vega's observation "The Resurrection is still happening, and you and I see evidence of it all around us, and even within us." **Ask:**

- Where do you see evidence of the Resurrection?
  ◊ within your congregation?
  ◊ within your community?
  ◊ around the world?

Remind the group of the question in the previous session, "Whom will you love?" and **ask:**

- How does obeying Jesus's instruction to "love your enemies" open the door for resurrection and new life?

Call attention to the section of *Questions Jesus Asked* titled "Your Mission in Life" and the three missions identified by Richard Bolles. **Ask:**

- What is the first mission?

- Where are you in the process of knowing your Creator and being conscious of God's presence every day?
- What is the second mission?
- What are you doing to make the world a better place?
- How are you joining other believers in the work of transforming your community so it is "in line with the kingdom of God"?

Invite a volunteer to read the description about the third mission from *Questions Jesus Asked.*

Note that sometimes an individual's unique mission is the same as his or her career but this is not always the case. Sometimes an individual will have a career in one field and fulfill his or her unique mission for God in another way.

Distribute paper and pencils or pens. **Say:**

We are going to have a few minutes for quiet reflection as we think about the questions related to the third mission and what we sense God calling us to do.

Feel free to make notes about the insights that come to you.

After you ask each of the following questions, allow a few minutes for quiet reflection before asking the next question.

Ask:

- What talents do you have that you can use for the kingdom of God?
- What places of service and settings for ministry appeal to you most?
- What needs can you meet using your talents in the places and settings that appeal to you?
- How are you already fulfilling the mission to which God has called you?
- What questions do you have about your unique mission?
- Do you feel God calling you to a new mission?

After this time of quiet reflection, invite volunteers to share their discoveries. If you have a large group, invite participants to share in pairs or small groups of three to four people.

Optional Activity: Questions Jesus Asked

This Optional Activity offers participants an opportunity to review and reflect on the six questions that have been the focus of this study.

Invite participants to turn to the list of questions in the Contents in *Questions Jesus Asked*.

Ask:

- How have your responses to any of these questions changed during the course of this study?
- How have you grown stronger in your faith and closer to the Lord during the course of this study?
- Which questions do you feel you need to consider in more depth?

Point out that it is helpful to come back to these questions frequently as we grow and mature in our faith.

Wrapping Up

Closing Activity

Review the list of responses to the question, "What are you looking for?" from the "Leading into the Study" activity.

Ask the question again, "What are you looking for?" and offer more time for volunteers to expand on their answers.

Review the meaning of the word *abide* (from the section "Where Are You Staying?").

Ask the Reflection question at the end of chapter 6 in *Questions Jesus Asked*: "What would abiding in Jesus look like for you?"

Remind the group of the "Leading into the Study" discussion from session 1 and these two Questions for Reflection:

- What concerns do you bring to this survey of questions Jesus asks of you?
- What do you hope emerges from this study for spiritual life and your commitment to Jesus?

Show the paper with the group's responses to these questions at the beginning of the study. Ask:

- How have your concerns been addressed and your hopes been fulfilled?
- What concerns and hopes do you have moving forward?

Closing Prayer

Close your time together with the following prayer or offer one of your own.

Loving and ever-present God, thank you for inviting us into your presence and calling us to serve you. Help us find the areas of ministry where we may best use our talents and abilities in the places and settings that appeal to us. Thank you for your faithful love, your redeeming grace, and the gift of eternal hope; in the name of your Son, Jesus Christ. Amen.

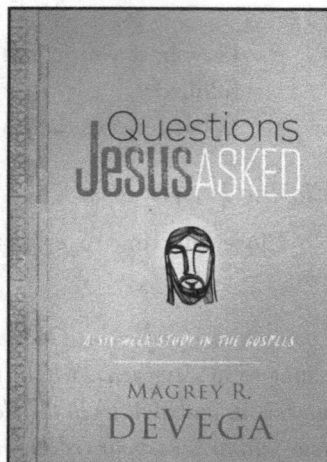

www.ingramcontent.com/pod-product-compliance
Lightning Source LLC
Chambersburg PA
CBHW010858090426
42737CB00020B/3416